MW01230420

Pieces Of Me

Written by Stormii Knight

Cover design by Kevon Knight

Edited by Candace Stewart, Collab Network, LLC

Black & Bare Press

For information, contact us at contact@blacknbarepress.com

Published by Black & Bare, LLC

Press Names: Stormii Knight, author.

Title: Pieces Of Me / Stormii Knight

www.blacknbarepress.com

Acknowledgments

I first have to thank God for his saving grace! Where would I be without Him! I would also like to acknowledge all the people who passed through my life. Goodand bad. A special thank you to those who have remained for playing your part in making me who I am. Whether you sowed into me or took pieces of me, those were lessons I needed to grow.

To my mother and father, who were polar.opposites yetthe same. Thank you for life.

To my grandmothers, who loved me differently but equally as much, I miss your love and care so much! You loved me, took care of me, and taught me many life lessons I am eternally grateful for.

To my beautiful children, I love you to life! Through all the trials and tribulations life threw our way, we have survived victoriously!

To my grandchildren, great-grandchildren, and all thoseto come, know that I love you and pray for you always!

Table of Contents

Pieces Of Me

SKY

Huge, fluffy, billowy clouds

sailing Gliding softly by

In the blue ocean of the sky

Holding within its core Cargo

that we need

What will it be this time?

Snow? Rain? Hail or seed? Oh,

how wondrous

God made the heavens

How wondrous he made the Earth How

wonderful it is that

we get to enjoy the joy of

each day that he gives birth from the

yellow of the daffodils

to the azure of the sea

God created all of this

Just for you

and me!

Again

I awaken

as if out of a dream

Slowly, I open my eyesto

see the moon rays

seeping through the window

falling across our bodies

I feel the softness of your manhood

against my thigh

reminding me of what was

just a few hours ago

Remembering the total, complete ecstasy

that was briefly mine

For when you awaken,

we will dress and leave here

Each to our own respective homes
and lie, yet again

About where we have been,

what we have done,

and who we were with It

it is better this way

We give to each other

what we can't get at home
Something that we're not willing to give

up, but neither of us wants to keep

So, we will keep meeting,

fulfilling our needs, and

giving up what we want so

no one will be hurt

Leave Me Alone

Why is it that you seem to show up

just as I'm getting my shit together?

Didn't you cause enough pain

in my life when we were together?

What is it that drives you

to continually taunt and harass me?

Is it not enough that you

had to spend twenty-five years

of your life behind bars for what you

did?

I divorced you.

DIVORCED YOU, DAMN IT!

Please, leave me alone

I have no space for you

in my life.

YES,

MY LIFE!

You saw to it

that there would

Never

Again

be a me and you

when you committed your crime.

Your crime!

That was the choice You made

and a choice you will have to live with

But one we all

Had to pay for.

Remember, I was forced to

deal with your choice

I just hope you've learned

something from all this

but I doubt that you have

It has been twelve long years

since I sent you to prison

And I hope it will be twelve more

before they let you out of there

You see, you need to know what

it is like to be broken

You need to

know whatit is like to be

betrayed

by someone you love

You need to

Know

what it feels like to lose

faith in humanity

and not know if you will

ever be the same again

To not know if you will ever be

able to

love,

trust,

or

see things through rose-colored glasses

again

You need to experience that so

you can have some idea

of the living hell that you put me

through

Don't get me wrong

I don't think you could ever do enough

timeto pay for what you did

You couldn't possiblydo

that many years

You wouldn't live long

enough But, just to set

the record straightI have a life

and I don't plan on spending it

wondering whether or not

you are rotting in that cell

If I had my way, that would have

happened a long time ago

But it is not my decision

it is God's

And his decision

is the one that counts

So, keep me

OUT

of your thought

I do not need to know that you

still exist

Let your wife be the recipient

of your pathetic, meaningless,

trivialattempts to declare your love

See, I know that you

really don't know anything about

loveYou don't love yourself

How could you possibly love anyone else?

Let me and mine alone

Go where you must

but don't let your path cross

mine

I am fine now, and I

intend to stay that way

I will keep living, keep

loving, and keep enjoying

life

despite

the pain

you caused me

Silent Rain

Silent rain falls against

the windowpane of my soul

slowly wearing away

the outer shell of my

being Each drop

penetrating the years of

pain, hurt, disappointment,

disillusionment, disgust,

betrayal,

jealousy, mistrust, and

deceit

Each drop

invites the warmth

of the outer world

in

one

tiny

drop

at

a

time

closer to

the

ice cold core

within
Each drop that

falls away

takes with it

the baggage
and regrets
of yesteryears
The silent rain stops
in the distance,
a rainbow in the
making is seen just
beyond the
horizon of life
Gently pushing its
way through
to turn the
rain

left behind into
prisms
of life
and light

New Age Love

You like the deep, dark, chocolate,

caramel of my skin

The velvety softness that is easily excited beneath your fingertips

The scent and taste

you can't seem to get enough of

You delight in my intelligence

In awe of the knowledge

stored in my brain

Wondering time and time

again, how could this be?

Wishing that you had discovered me

sooner but,

knowing that it would

have never been allowed

then

It would have had to be

a secret love

Known only to

you

and me

You would not have had the courage it took

for us

to exist

as one

Then, I would have had to

bear the pain of love known

and not to have

as I looked at you

each and every day

with another by your side

That was then

This is

now

Oh, how things have

changed

The power lies

with me now

You repeatedly ask, when will I meet those most

important in your life?

I answer honestly and say I don't know

There are so many things that I

need to consider

I am strong enough to make the decision

and live with it, are you?

Do you still harbor fear of

not being like the others?

Are you strong enough to love, honor,

cherish, and protect me?

Protect Me!

Protect me from the hateful glares,

the snide remarks,

the blatant disrespect

to come our way just because we have chosen to love one

another and embrace our likeness

as well as our differences?

What you embrace wholeheartedly and unconditionally

behind closed doors,

Can you do that with the rest of the world?

Yes, baby, I know you can and will

do whatever it takes to make me happy, keep me

happy It is my fear of what the world

around us has cheated us of already

and what it might try to take away

Mama

Mama, I need you

Now

I need your love, care,

patience, guidance, and

teaching

I still love you, mama

My love is unconditional

I will always remember

that you would abandon me

At the first hint of a man

wanting to pay

some

attention

to you

or your friends

wanting to spend

a wild night,

weekend,

or

Week

Sometimes

Weeks

Partying

It didn't matter that you

had no money or three

children They took you

along

because you were the life of

the party, and they would

have more fun

with you there
It was your chance

to escape the real world of the

eighteen-year-old mother of

three

who were all under

three for that

night, weekend, or week

which eventually turned into

weeks
and months

of not seeing

or hearing from you

mama

But I still love you mama

and I need for you to

love me,

care for me, want me,

miss me,

and long for me to be there

when I'm not with you Like, I

miss you

and cry

for you

each time

you leave

never knowing when,

or if

I will ever see you again

I love you, mama

My love is unconditional

I need your love to be

unconditional too

You see

I didn't ask to come here You

brought me here because

satisfaction, pleasure, and not

caution was more important to

you You brought me here

so please, do right by me I

love you, mama

My love is

unconditional

I'm Sorry

I

Wasnt

What

You

were looking for

but you never

thought about

the consequences

of your pleasure

times three

So, here we are

mama

waiting on you

to love

us

unconditionally

Too

Look At Me

Look at me
Look at me good

Tell me,
what is it
that makes you uncomfortable
about how I look?
What hidden insecurities do
you harbor
that make you
want to lash out at me,
hurt me,

talk about me?
Chances are
you don't even know me

If you gave yourself half a
chance

you would like me

probably become a friend.

What

makes

you

think

that you are so much better

than me

that you

try to diss me?

Degrade me?

Yeah, I may be different

from you

But that does

not give you the right

to trespass

on my feelings,

or into my world

Uninvited

I could probably look at you and

say some hurtful things but is it

worth it?

Is it worth it to hurt

someone you don't even

know?

Why not try being a

Little kinder,

More understanding,

even tolerant

of others

You just may discover

what it is

you

don't

like

about

yourself

and fix it

Execution

I watched

as they led him away

handcuffs around his wrists,

chains around his ankles

I stood there, real still

Watching him look back at me

with those big ol' eyes

shining bright with tears

he wouldn't let his eyelids spill

Because he thought

I wanted him

to be strong for me

He was showing me

he was still a man

even though

he would be nothing

in a few minutes

I didn't want him to

hold

back

the tears

I didn't

want him to be strong

for me

or him,

for that matter

I wanted him to

break away

from those prison guards

To yell

and scream

at the top of his voice

I DIDN'T DO IT!

I DON'T DESERVE TO

DIE! PLEASE!

Don't make me your sacrificial

lamb

I wanted him to break away and

run to me

Throw his arms around me and

squeeze me

with all his might

and then tell me he loved me

I wanted him to cry

God!

how I wanted him to

acknowledge the pain,

hurt,

and injustice he felt

I didn't want to stand still looking at him
going down

that corridor

He wouldn't be walking back down

That noise

That screaming

That yelling and moaning

Why won't it stop?!

Because I can't let it!

Ending This Thing...

I sit here alone yet
with you Looking
out
of the window
wishing I was anywhere
but here
I feel the warmth of
your body next to
mine
The strength of
your arms

as
they
enfold
me
I glance around the room

and see All

that

You

have given me

Because of

You

there is Nothing

I could ever want
You have given me all that

lies within these walls,

except you

I never will have you

You belong

to someone else
Each time I try to leave you

find a reason to stay

You profess your undying love

and

commitment

Something that you have

never been able to give

your wife

What would she say

if she knew about me?

Would it then be so hard for

you to leave?

This

thing

has gone on much

too

long

One

of

us

needs to have

the strength to leave

And since

you say

it

is

Not

going to be You

then I guess

it will have to be

Me

Cheap Lesson

You allowed him to take me on his lap when I was

eleven

saying, go on

and get some of that

money from daddy man

Couldn't you see?

Look, he wants to give you more

than he's giving the others, you said

While he doled out pennies and

nickels to the other children,

he waved dollar bills at me

I tried not to go, fought

not to go I knew the cost

I cried, screamed, and yelled not to go

Afraid of his tongue, hands,

and the

things he would do to me while you

slept

but you pushed me forward anyway

Did you know what that dollar-cost

me?

Did you care?

Alone

I feel a cold dark wind
blowing around me, through me I
see nothing
It is so dark here I can
feel it
It is so empty I can taste it
There is no smell
yet my nostrils fill
with the rancid nothingness
The silence
is so deep
my ears feel as though I'm
standing at the
bottom of an empty well in
the middle of a
black and barren

night ridden desert

I

Am

Alone...

USED

I was a number, you
used me... Added me
to your lengthy
list of has-beens and
wannabes who still
linger for just a little
bit of your
love Excuse me, lust...
Trickery and deceit are
the tools
by
which you
gain entrance to
places you
would
not

normally

have

access

to...

Once granted entrance

you ravage and devour

all that is in your path

And once your

gluttonous appetite

is

sated

and you

are done dining,

you leave behind

nothing but an

empty shell

HOPE

I offered you peace at every turn
you didn't accept it
Instead, you choose to continue
in that deep, dark, hellish pit of
despair, self-pity, sorrow, and blame
When will you stop castrating
yourself? Decide to live, save yourself,
and
redeem
your life...
End this
dizzying
spiral
into
the hell,
that

is

your

past...

You

can

win,

but you must want to

You must fight

let go of the negativity

that you

allow

to hold you captive

I can offer you no more

Lest I follow you

into

the depths of darkness

As for me,

I have chosen

a different path

I have chosen to

struggle,

climb, fall, and continue to

climb

until I reach daylight

once more...

Lay down your burdens and

follow me

WHY? WHY? WHY?

My soul cries out Why

can't they see? Why

can't they feel?

Why don't they try to know?

The things I know

The things I feel

Why don't they try to see

the reality in the world around us?

Why can't we stop hating,

hurting, and killing each other?

Why can't we learn to live

in the world together

and learn to respect

each other? Why?

Why must life be so cruel?

What kind of world is this that

doesn't allow a man to cry?

yet takes delight

in a woman's tears?

We are all human

We all cry

We all hurt

We all bleed red blood,

feel sorrow, pain, and

despair What kind of world

is this that won't stop the

violence?

Yeah, I know they say they are

trying

But, when,

and how?

And trying for who?

My soul will continue to cry out

with a wail so loud and so long

For some justice for

Just us

Love Is

Love is a tumultuous emotion
that starts like a wild
roller coaster ride
with its many highs and lows
twist and turns
Sudden changes of
direction pulling you up
and down
in and out
around and

around until
you learn to ride or
get off

Confetti

Confetti falls

all around me

Yet,

it is

not

a joyous occasion

Each piece

represents

a tiny portion

Of my heart

blown into the wind Never

to

return

You & Me

I just want to be held
Sometimes....
I want to be at home
lying in your arms
with the warmth of your body
enveloping me
radiating into mine...
I want to hold your arms
as you gently move the hair
away from my neck

and kiss me...
I want to look up into your
smiling face
as your arms surround
my waist
holding me oh so close...

I want to hold your hand as

we talk and talk...

Taking the time to

discuss everything and

nothing

enjoying the time that we have

together... I want so much...

But most of all...

I just want to be with you.

Come love and lay with me

Gaze with me into that deep

blue sea called the sky

Where the moon is held high,

so high above the Earth mixed

with the stars

It generates thoughts of love

and being with you

through thick and thin or is
it thin and thick
Whatever, whichever I am to be,
me with you
and you with me
All ways, all days, and
nights too I'd like to be
with you in every way every
day through eternity

Come Lay With Me

Come love and lay with me

Gaze with me

Into that deep

Blue sea

Called the sky

Where the moon is held high

So high above the Earth

Mixed with stars

It generates thoughts of love

And being with you through thick and thin

Or is it thin and thick

Whatever

Whichever

I am to be me with you

All ways

All days

And nights too

I'd like to be with you

In every Way

Every Day

Through eternity

What Kind Of World Is This?

What kind of world is this?

That would allow people

To think that it's okay for them

To chain a man to a truck and

Drag him to his death

What kind of world is this?

That would allow police,

Our protectors, to kill

For no good reason

Without consequence

What kind of world is this?

That allows little

children

to Taunt

and

slang racial slurs

At other little children

Because

their parents have taught them

That they are better

and more Privileged than

anyone else

And no one tries to

Correct this injustice

What kind of world

Is this

that takes care of the rich

and famous

And

allows

the

poor

to

suffer

and

die?

It Wasn't So Long Ago

You know

It wasn't so long ago that I was in your

shoes,

Hopes,

dreams,

aspirations...

So many words unspoken

So many songs unsung

You know

It wasn't so long ago

that I wanted to soar...

Fly high

up above the clouds,

Lingering in the air,

Never

wanting to return

to this hell

they call Earth,

But knowing that I must.

For if I didn't, I wouldn't be able to be

here

For you...

To help

you Lead

you Guide you

Because I can remember

That not long ago that it was

me

Needing Help

Love

Guidance

Hope

Praying

That someone

Anyone

Would remember

Me

Lay Me Down

Lay me down
Slowly, gently Take
good care of my
heart
My love,
my being,
my soul
Look deep
into my eyes
See the
passion that is held
within me
for only you Take my
lips
with care and with
gentle passion Wrap

your warm, loving

arms around me and

take

me

with total,

uninhibited

passion

Letter to an Ex-lover

A thousand thoughts swirl in the misty recesses of my mind. As my brain plays the tape of that not too sweet romance that once was. I wonder if you ever knew what I truly thought of you. I won-der if you ever really valued the unconditional love that I so freely gave? Did it ever matter that I often sacrificed many things for you just because you were my man, and I would do whatever it took to make sure you succeeded? I wonder now as I contemplate the yesteryears and the not so long-ago yesterday's, why didn't we end it sooner? I think a lot of it was my willingness and determination to succeed, succeed at all costs. One lesson that I have thoroughly learned from all this is that it is okay to lose. Sometimes, when you lose, you are really winning, even though it may not seem like it at the time. You eventually come to the realization it was meant to be, and you are now better off. I hope you are okay, and I want us to continue to communicate. We were such good friends; too bad we couldn't make it work. What started so right ended up all wrong, but at least we were able to salvage our friendship. So, goodbye, and good luck and I'll talk to you soon

Six Years Ago

Time gone Never

to return

Yet

I

see evidence

of

your existence

In

a

faded

picture

and the worn pages of a diary

With too many

tear-stained pages

And too few expressions of

love,

laughter,

and joy

Still, you were there...

And remain here today

As I look at

the words that flow

effortlessly from my

pen

I notice

not

much

has

changed...

FEEL GOOD MAN

Ooooh...

You made me

feel like a real woman

Buying me gifts giving

me money Hell... I didn't

even ask you to

You just did it because

you knewthat's what a

man is supposed to do

(You said and I thought)

You massaged my mind

as well

as my body Licked my

toes

Some

other

things

too!

Ooooh, child...

You cleaned my house

And cooked my meals

(I thought I had died and gone to

Heaven!)

And Even

Washed my clothes

Worked

not one, but two jobs

You were perfect Then,

I found out

I wasn't the only one

Damn!

Why does it always have to

be the good ones?

Shattered Pieces

Shattered

pieces

The sticky feel

of blood

On broken glass

As I

try

to repair

The

jigsaw puzzle

Of

a

broken heart

You

You gave me
what I thought I wanted
You took the time
to make me feel special You
showered me
with unending notes,
cards, and letters You
caressed me Mind, body,
and soul You were such
a gentleman
You paid attention to my
needs
You did what you
needed to do to get
what you wanted

Now,

you are gone and

here we are without

you...

SUSPENDED

I lay here suspended in time

And space,

in this universe

I lay here with my thoughts, my feelings, and

emotions Suspended in the air that surrounds

me

I lay here with the electrical charges of each synapse

paused midway

Between the negative and positive poles of my brain

I have reached that oh too familiar place called the

decision Where the heart wants to rule against better

judgment

The place where it is excruciatingly difficult to let the

ties that bind loose

So that freedom can be rediscovered and the sweet

melancholy thoughts

Of being yourself and independent return
I lay here suspended in space and time,

all at the same time

Because to choose is frightening and exciting meshed

together

in one tiny molecule that can explode and fragment

my world as I now know it

To choose means either life or death for a

part of me

Life for the person I know I am capable of

being

the part of me that has not been allowed to blossom

and grow into something useful and beautiful

Death for the part of me that is comfortable being

where it has no business being

I lay here suspended in space

Vacillating between the frailty of my heart and the

intelligence of my brain

So, I continue to lay here suspended in space with

a choice to make

SOUL FOOD RESTAURANT

It's the place you go to feed
Not only your body but your soul
It's the place you go to meet and greet

People young and old
Church goer's,
wino's
Regular people too

The soul food restaurant
Is just the place to find good food
People standing all about
In the hot summer sun
Waiting in line for

Good times, food, and fun

It's easy to get caught up in

the colorful menagerie

Laughter, talking, dancing

Games of life of and play

From the two little girls on the street

Playing old Mary Mack

To the old man in the parking lot

Dancing, yelling, and shouting,

"Get back!"

Neighborhood boy's running around

playing ball

Old women gathered, talking, and

gossiping

If you need to know or have it told, they will

do it all

Young men hustling for their daily bread

Young women hustling for just enough to

be fed

The soul food restaurant is the place you

want to go to get the food for your body

But also feed your soul

IF YOU'RE NOT HERE TOMORROW

If you're not here tomorrow
The clouds will continue to be in the sky
The sun will continue to rise in the east and set in
the west The moon will continue to have its
beautiful glow
And the stars will continue to shine ever so brightly

If you're not here tomorrow
The wind will continue to gently
blow The trees will stand tall and
green Casting their shade
everywhere
And the waves of the ocean will roll gently to shore

If you're not here tomorrow
The flowers will continue
to bloom

And the birds will continue to

sing

Bringing a smile to faces here and there

If you're not here tomorrow
Surely my heart will feel as if it's been

broken into a thousand pieces that will

never mend With no hope of ever being

whole again

I will feel the pain of love gained and

lost Half of this whole gone

Never to be replaced
I will shed a million tears

And isolate myself and my

feelings for days on end

For if you're not here tomorrow

I will know that with each pain a cost is

paid

And behind every dark cloud lies a

rainbow

For if you're not here tomorrow I

will

I must go on

QUIET SERENITY

I feel the gentle touches of rain
as the drops slowly fall from the
blue-gray sky against my upturned
brown face caressing me from head to toe
I hear the sweet melodic sounds of raindrops
as they fall against the trees, flowers, barn, car,
my skin A tin roof somewhere off in the distance
echoes the lazy rain sounds and tries to
lull me into a peaceful state of mind
I watch the growing grass climbing taller,
flowers open their cups to quench their
thirst,
the Earth that soaks up all it can to
cease its drought, and save some for a not so
rainy day
I feel the rain like a lover's hand

moving deftly against my

skin Gentle, yet hard

Persistent yet cautious

The continuous perfect

rhythm of what is to be

whether we want it or not

SOAR

Why did I stay?
I asked myself
a thousand times
Why did I
let you torture
my body and my mind? I
married you out of what I
thought was love

And then, found out this
was something you knew
nothing of
A million excuses
I made to stay
by your side
Denying to myself
what I knew

were obvious lies
I wanted this love thing to work and

to have you as my husband for life

To care for your children,

whom I gave birth

I just assumed I'd always be your wife

Then you raised your hand one time too

many That's when I decided that I had had

plenty

I packed up my children

Left all I had behind

For I knew a new life I

had to find

You kept calling cause
you thought it would be just like before

You would cry,

apologize,

make promises, and see me come back

through that door

I am now someone that loves you no more

who can see that my life has much

more in store

So all your

self-hate and

insecurities

I'm leaving behind

For me and my children, a new

life I will find

BROWN FANTASY

A beautiful, brown body

Appears on the screen

Tattoos and braids

Tall, long, and lean

Beautiful, brown eyes,

Made to look just at me!

The velvet of his skin,

Those sensuous lips,

The picture I stare at

That stops just above his hips. I

long to see more

But this vision eludes my eyes.

Oh! What I

would give,

For just one ride on those thighs!

The promises he speaks of

For the thrill of one night
If he told me those premises
Were for me
I'd be on the
next flight! "How does it
feel?", He asks Well, I want
to know
And I'm sure he would
Leave me begging for
more
But then,
maybe it
Would be he
Who would be
begging me,
Because I'm no slouch
When it comes to pleasing

My man

A kiss here, a touch there

And feeling my tongue

You know...

Everywhere Brown

sugar babe

I guess I'll have to pass

For

my

man

knows

what

I

want

And

that's

a

love

that

will

last

Truth

No one likes to stare truth in the
face It's cold, hard, and ugly
No one likes to stare truth in the
face It makes you uncomfortable
Truth is unrelenting and unforgiving
No one likes to stare truth in the face
It forces you to look at the realities around
you
Forcing you to trade in those rose-colored
glasses
For clear lens so that nothing is hidden from
view
No one likes to stare truth in the face
For it tells us all we do not want to
know

Bidding us to look beyond the surface

And to dig deep

within the soul

No one likes to stare truth in the face

For our realities are not always what's

true Truth tells us the niche that we've

carved out for ourselves are u little

overblown,

Over Exaggerated and pompous

No one likes to stare truth in the face

It will cause us to seek what we don't want to

find Making our good lives seem somehow

unpleasant

No one likes to stare truth in the

face

But we must learn to

With truth comes power,

knowledge, self-respect, understanding and

compassion

No one likes to stare truth in the

face

But with truth,

We find our space

Love?

I lay here thinking

I can't remember the last time we

touched

The last time we kissed

The last time we said

any kind words to one another

or the last time we made love We

exist here with one another yet

we are here alone

each in our own space

daring the other to invade

We don't belong together

yet there is so much between us

There are

good memories and bad

some memories that we will never

forget and those we wish we never had

What are we going to do?

We can't go on living like this

I don't trust you

You don't trust me

There is no real love between us

We have just gotten used to one another

that makes it easy for us to continue to coexist

even though it is difficult at best to be civil to

one another

What will it take to discontinue this

charade?

Which of the two of us will have the guts to

make the decision that so obviously has to

be made I keep telling myself it's because of

the children

What

will

they do

without him?

So, I suffer so that they will be

whole You say they need a

mother

and continue to live in unhappiness

so that their still fragile

development will continue to grow

We owe it to them

to not be

selfish

and think about our own pressing desires,

or do we?

I Know Love

I hear the silence of love not yet quite known

I see the misery of love gained and lost

I see the touch of love that comes from connecting with
another

I taste every word that flows effortlessly from my
mouth

I smell the sweet, wonderful, sensual aroma of love as

we find each other with caution and abandon

I know love, I receive love, and I give love

Here we are, once again

Here we are once again

At the place where love began

Trying to sort out what went

wrong

Grasping at straws

to keep love strong Knowing inside

that it won't work

And if we stay together

Someone will get hurt

I look at the place where we first began

It could have never worked,

Because it started in sin

If we want a love that's real

We must begin with what is real

Leaving all wants and desires

behind

To find what's right, good, and

kind

Putting God first and while all else

follows Guarantees our life will not be

hollow

"ON OUR DAY"

I may not be the prettiest package

Fashioned with glitter or gold

Nor am I the most captivating

Still yet your heart I hold

I don't have riches or treasures

For all the world to see

All I have is love, kindness, and

pleasure To give and for you to receive

You looked past the outer me

You dared to go deep inside Told

me what you found there Was

worth more than any prize

Dignity,

esteem,

and

self-respect

Are

what

you encountered within Loyalty,

trust,

humility,

and even a little sin

No, I am not perfect

But you choose to love me still

And on that day when you say I

do I shall say, I will

Just One Look

Just one look
and you had me hooked

The beauty in your soul was
more than I could hold

The passion in your eyes
held me mesmerized
The touch of your hand let
me know that
you were more than a man
Surely much more than this
woman could stand
The heat blowing softly from
your lips unto mine
made me forget all sense of
direction and time

Is this what love is like?

I've never felt this way before cause if it is, I want to feel like this forevermore

Moonlit highs and river lows

how you enchanted me only God

knows

The swells in your arms

as they encircle my waist

The sweet thickness of your

tongue as you give me a taste

Of that deep dark chocolate

that flows from deep within

If I play my cards right

your family will be calling

me kin In the moment right

next to you is where I always

want to be with you stroking

my thighs

and caressing my
back
For my love for you
knows no lack
For the love you give to me
you will
receive much in return
An honest heart full of love
and loyalty to burn
For what you've given to me
I can never repay
And I plan on seeing that it
stays that way
Love like this is a one-time
thing
And the words of this song
are to let you know how much
joy

you bring

From this day forth

together we will be

And I intend to always let

you know just

how much

you

mean

to me

Feelings

Allow your arms to enfold
my body into yours
Holding me so close that
two hearts unite
and beat as one
Let the gentle heat of your
breath warm my soul
as it blows gently into my ear
Let the soft coarseness
of your ample lips play
wantonly
at my neckline
as your teeth pull gently at
my blouse
The sweet soft thickness of
your tongue

causes me to shiver and

to think

of what else you might

do with your tongue

or what I might do with

mine Then you slowly

turn me around and

ask, "Now?"

And I answer, "Yes" The

wait is over Because

I know

That

this

is

Love

One More Day

A weary head
lays upon my breast
I stroke his hair gently
trying to wipe away
all the pain of this day and the days
before hoping that he will
make it through yet another day
It is not easy
watching him
day after day after day
carrying the burdens
that he must
just to
make it one more
day

I Have Been

I have been smashed, hammered,
beaten, and broken
by those, I thought loved me
Family, friends, lovers, and the
like
who professed their loyalty and love
Who constantly took and gave nothing in
return My safe house became a den of terror
Fear became my best friend
While self-hate ran a close second
with doubts and disdain
My tears that fell like rain
would leave me empty
Unable to give or receive
Wanting to love but not able to I
had been through too much it

was too painful

but I kept smiling

If you looked close enough you would see that I was empty

unable to give or receive

Wanting to love but not able to

I had been though too much

it was too painful, but I kept smiling

If you looked close enough you could see the sadness in my eyes

just past the smile on my lips

were tears ready to spill over

at

any

moment

and create an ocean

that would release some of the pain

If only for a little while

Butterfly

Big warm, beautiful hands

All over my body

They float so easily

Around me

It feels like

Butterflies

Softly

Kissing me

All over

I never knew

A man's touch

Could convey

so much

I never knew

You knew so much about

When to touch

How to touch Where to touch

I still feel that

Just gently there

Sensation

Floating

Ever so softly

Around me

Just

like

a

Butterfly

Dedication to my Daddy

Daddy, you taught me

Love, laughter, caring,

Dignity and respect You

taught me to

Pick up the pieces When

things fell apart You

showed me

Not all men are dogs

You taught me

That I deserved

someone Who

could love, cherish,

Honor, respect, and support me I

learned from you that

not only do little boys

need a father

but that little girls also
need a father present
in their lives
I watched you
teach the young men
in our community
how to become men
I heard you tell them to
always Love, respect,
and protect Their
queens,
Nurture and guide
their young
I saw you reach out to
many
And tell all who would
listen How great God's
love is How

important it is to keep

God first

But most of all, daddy

You taught me

To be the woman

That I am

About the author

Born in Nashville, Tennessee, to an unwed teen mother, life had already thrown a curveball her way. Life for Stormii would be anything but easy. Coming of age in the south was no easy task for a child of color inthe sixties. Being raised in the midst of the civil rights movement was sure to leave an indelible mark on the heart and mind of a young black female child.

Stormii witnessed and experienced many prejudices and miscarriages of justice personally and publicly while growing up in Nashville.

Although Nashville was her birthplace, life circumstances would allow her to travel and experience even moreof the world. The moves to other places outside Tennessee were not of her choosing. Life necessitatedthat it be.

Discovering reading early in life was a means of escape from the ugly reality of

the world around her.

From reading, writing was a natural progression.

The saving grace was her grandmother. A woman imemersed deep in family, faith, and a woman who loved Stormii unconditionally. It was her who instilled in her a love for God, reading, writing, nature, and people.

She taught Stormii not one person was more important than another. Whether it is the president or a person onthe street, they each deserve the same respect.

Although life knocked her down more than a few times, she did what her grandmother taught her to do.

Keep getting up, never stop trying, and keep faith in God!

Made in the USA
Columbia, SC
12 November 2021

48532877R00076